"In this lively and lucid little book, Michael Wagenman teaches the book of Acts under the conviction that God is a missionary God who intends for his people to be a missionary people. Under the leadership of Christ and the empowerment of the Spirit, we, his people, are called to bring our neighbors and indeed entire societies into a missionary encounter with the gospel. Highly recommended."

—Bruce Ashford, author of *Every Square Inch* and *One Nation Under God*

"Fresh and refreshing—a new look at Acts for everyone from amateur Bible students to biblical scholars."

—Leith Anderson, president, National Association of Evangelicals, Washington, D.C.

"Wagenman successfully displays the unique role of Acts within the Bible, rescues us from a tired reading of Scripture, and helps us to hear its message with fresh ears. Though [Acts is] a well-worn narrative in many churches, *Together for the World* brings [the book] to life in its ancient and modern contexts, helping the reader to behold Luke's magisterial aims—literally and literarily."

—Dru Johnson, professor of biblical and theological studies, The King's College

T0341391

TOGETHER FOR THE WORLD

THE BOOK OF ACTS

**Other titles in
the Transformative Word series:**

TOGETHER FOR THE WORLD

THE BOOK OF ACTS

TRANSFORMATIVE WORD

MICHAEL R. WAGENMAN

Edited by Craig G. Bartholomew

LEXHAM PRESS

Lexham Press, 1313 Commercial St., Bellingham, WA 98225
LexhamPress.com

Print ISBN 9781577997191
Digital ISBN 9781577997207

Series Editor: Craig G. Bartholomew
Lexham Editorial Team: Lynnea Fraser, Abby Salinger,
    Abigail Stocker
Cover Design: Brittany Schrock
Back Cover Design: Liz Donovan
Typesetting: ProjectLuz.com

TABLE OF CONTENTS

INTRODUCTION

A public art installation created by Pieterjan Gijs sits 80 kilometers outside of Brussels, Belgium. From a distance, it appears to be a little church building atop a small countryside hill; but *this* church is constructed of rows of rusty steel beams separated by gaps—an optical illusion. Depending on where you stand, the church either appears or fades from view; from one angle, the building is nearly invisible, and from another angle it reappears. And if you stand within the structure, your view of the outside world is either completely obstructed or virtually uninhibited.

Figure 1 - Copyright Filip DuJardin. Used by permission.

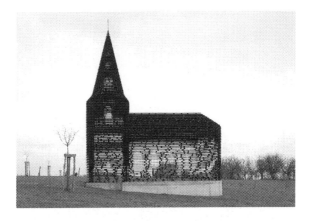

Figure 2 - Copyright Filip DuJardin. Used by permission.

Figure 3 - Copyright Filip DuJardin. Used by permission.

From some angles, you can also see the nearby city in the background, with an old church standing in the center of the community. Which of these two buildings represents the place of the church today: the one in the center of the community, or the one physically disconnected from it, nearly invisible? Is the church today a centrally located beacon and point of reference, or invisible, marginal, and disconnected from the heart of community life?

Figure 4 - Copyright Filip DuJardin. Used by permission.

The sculpture visually depicts a key tension facing the church today. Where does the church of Jesus Christ stand in the 21st century? What is its role within such a religiously diverse society? How should the church relate to other civic institutions, particularly the state government? How should Christians respond to ridicule, insult, rejection, and persecution? Should the church try to reclaim a central place in society, or accept marginalization?

The first-century church asked these same questions. We often imagine biblical times as far away and long ago, but reading the book of Acts reminds us that many of the issues and questions facing the church haven't changed since the very beginning.

God can use Acts to transform your life and the life of your church today. Acts isn't just about the dynamic people of God in history; Acts is about *the ongoing means* by which God is still transforming people to be his witnesses in the world. The book not only narrates the spread of the gospel by the Holy Spirit and the apostles but shows the church proclaiming the gospel, oriented to the world and working for the world's healing and redemption.

> Acts is about the ongoing means by which God is still transforming people to be his witnesses in the world.

Overview

Whenever I visit a new congregation that I'm interested in joining, I ask about their history. In response, I'm often told a story—complete with important people, dates, and events in the unfolding life of this particular gathering of people. The story is usually told chronologically, but it's intentionally crafted in light of the congregation's present identity. This makes sense: Our stories shape our identity and our place in the world.

When reading the book of Acts, the particular story it tells quickly becomes clear. Within the New Testament, Acts functions as the hinge between the Gospels and the letters.[1] Acts tells the story of how Jesus' ministry transitioned to the apostles, who, by the Holy Spirit's leading, announced the gospel of the kingdom of God to the first-century world.

The story of Acts begins in Jerusalem with Jesus and his disciples. The disciples receive the Holy Spirit and become apostles—the ones Jesus commissions to be foundational in proclaiming the message of salvation in his name. This proclamation begins in Jerusalem, primarily under Peter's leadership, in the vicinity of the temple, and moves outward to the rest of the world. Initially, they see great receptivity to the gospel message, but the situation quickly becomes deadly.

After the death of the apostle Stephen (Acts 7:54–60), the story of Acts shifts from Peter to a prominent Jewish Pharisee, Saul—who is determined, with religious zeal, to stamp out the "Jesus sect" within Judaism. But while traveling on this mission, he personally and dramatically encounters the risen Christ. Not only does his name change from Saul to Paul after this, but his life forever changes (Acts 9:1–18).

The Acts story then shifts back to Peter in Jerusalem, and then to Paul and the wider Roman Empire. The last two-thirds of Acts recounts Paul's missionary travels around the Mediterranean world as he preaches in Jewish synagogues and Gentile marketplaces. Paul encounters both resistance to and acceptance of the saving message of Jesus. Where his audience receives the gospel in faith—often in startling ways (miraculous healings, resurrections from the dead, and speaking in foreign tongues/languages)—he starts small house churches, which unify in a network around the Mediterranean by the end of his travels.

Acts closes with Paul's arrest by the Roman authorities—with help from the Jewish religious authorities, just like in Jesus' story—in Jerusalem and his journey to Rome (Acts 21:27–28:31). The authorities place Paul under house arrest, but he continues to preach the gospel without hindrance while awaiting trial (Acts 28:16–31).

As noted above, Acts is the link between the Gospels and the New Testament letters which follow it.

In particular, Acts has a special relationship with the Gospel of Luke. We notice this in the opening words of Acts 1:1: "In the first book ... " (There are other ancient documents written like this. For example, the ancient Jewish historian Josephus wrote a two-volume work, *Against Apion*, in which the second volume also begins, "In my first book ... ") The story of Acts is really the continuation of a much larger story; it's the second volume of Luke's two-volume work, which begins with Luke's Gospel (the topic of authorship will be discussed in more detail later).

Luke's Gospel tells the story of Jesus' ministry. The author opens Acts by picking up immediately where his Gospel left off: with Jesus' ascension and the coming of the Holy Spirit. Luke's Gospel is about what Jesus *began* to do, and Acts is about what Jesus *continued* to do—through his Spirit and the church. This is the "big picture" story of Acts. For this reason, it's important to read Acts within its context—especially within the context of Jesus' ministry, which brought God's promises in the Old Testament to fulfillment.

Outline

Contemporary readers of the Bible often forget (or don't realize) that the biblical authors, like other ancient authors, did not write with chapter and verse divisions. In fact, many manuscripts often left out spaces between words. So the process of dividing up words, sentences, paragraphs, verses, and chapters (not to mention inserting headings, subheadings, or footnotes) is a process of interpretation.

The same is true for the process of outlining biblical books. The interpreter's view of who wrote the book, to whom they wrote, and—most important— why they wrote all determine how he or she divides up and organizes the text's outline.

Although we could outline Acts based on its geography, important characters, or sermons—each of which highlights something important in the story— the most helpful outlines will follow the textual clues within Acts. We find the first clue in Acts 1:8, which records Jesus as saying that his disciples will be his witnesses "in Jerusalem, in all Judea and Samaria, and to the ends of the earth." The rest of Acts unfolds exactly along these geographic-cultural lines. The geographic expansion of the early church from Jerusalem to Rome is a major interpretive key for recognizing the organization—and purpose—of Acts.

A second clue can be found with the main disciples to whom Jesus passes the torch of gospel expansion as missionaries. In Acts 2–12, we meet Stephen and Philip, but the main focus remains on Peter. Similarly, in Acts 13–28, we meet Barnabas, Silas, Timothy, and others, but the main focus rests on Paul. As attention shifts from Peter to Paul, the gospel shifts further outward from Jerusalem into the world foreign to Jews.

A third clue is the role of religious and political authorities throughout the book of Acts. From the very beginning, the church must negotiate between religious persecution around the Jerusalem temple on the one side and rival political loyalties throughout the Roman colonies on the other. Luke goes to great lengths to point out that Jesus will build his church and nothing will be able to stop it (see Matt 16:18).

Theological Center

The theological center of Acts is the missionary nature of Christian faith under Jesus' commissioning leadership and the Holy Spirit's empowering presence. Acts reveals God as a missionary God, intent on redeeming all of creation. In order to accomplish this, Jesus came, died, and rose again to inaugurate the kingdom of God on earth. The apostles, through the leading of the Holy Spirit, are sent from Jerusalem to the ends of the known world with the gospel—the announcement that in Jesus, we can find forgiveness and new life. The church, therefore, is the initial realization of the kingdom of God in the world.[2] Christians are sent into the entire world to be Jesus Christ's ambassadors (2 Cor 5:20; Eph 6:20), the salt and light of the gospel (Matt 5:13–16). The church is a witness to what God has done, is doing, and will do.

But Acts isn't just a history lesson on the church's long-ago beginnings. No, before telling the human side of the story, Acts is primarily occupied with revealing the nature of the triune God, the power of the gospel to renew that which is rebellious against God, and the calling and mandate of the church in and for the world. Reading Acts today, therefore, is the means by which lives and churches may be transformed into God's dynamic people so the world can be transformed into the kingdom of God.

OUTLINE FOR THE BOOK OF ACTS

Acts 1–12   Peter and the Beginnings of the
               Church in Jerusalem/Judaea

   Acts 1–9:31   Jerusalem, Judaea,
                                     Galilee, and Samaria

   Acts 9:32–12   Phoenicia, Cyprus, and
                                       Antioch

Acts 13–28   Paul and the Expansion of the
               Church from Among the Nations

   Acts 13–15:35   Phrygia and Galatia

   Acts 15:36–21:16   Macedonia

   Acts 21:17–28:31   Rome

SUGGESTED READING

☐ For Luke's introduction to his two-volume
   work (Luke–Acts), read Luke 1:1–4.

☐ For background on Luke as Paul's
   companion, read Colossians 4:14;
   Philemon 24; and 2 Timothy 4:11.

☐ For more about the promise of the Holy
   Spirit, read Joel 2:28–29.

Reflection

What exposure have you already had to the book of Acts? What assumptions do you bring to your reading of it?

_____

_____

_____

When you hear the word "church," what do you think of? What has been your experience with church?

_____

_____

_____

If Acts was written as a form of gospel proclamation, how does that affect how it should be read—how do we proclaim the gospel today? What should be our posture as we read and teach the story of Acts?

_____

_____

_____

BACKGROUND TO ACTS

When you pick up the newspaper, how do you know the front-page news should be read differently than the political cartoon and still differently than the classifieds? Because you've learned that they're each a different type of literature, meant to be read differently. The same is true for reading poetry, a mystery novel, or an advertisement on the subway: If you don't distinguish between these different types of writing, you don't stand a chance of correctly understanding what you're reading. In this chapter, we'll discuss important background elements—genre, author, date, audience, and purpose—that will better equip you to read and understand the text of Acts.

Literary Traits

What kind of literature is Acts? Within these 28 chapters, we find a diversity of literary forms. There are sermons and speeches. There are numerous religious and political authorities who appear on the scene. We learn a lot about some key apostles' lives and the development of the early church through them.

We hear many contextualized presentations of the good news about Jesus—to Jews, Romans, and others. Through Paul's multiple missionary journeys, we are presented with a detailed Mediterranean travelogue. And there are bits of general first-century history and culture throughout. Placed between the Gospels and the letters, Acts is located at the New Testament's turning point.

Evangelical Cuban theologian Justo Gonzalez has observed that Acts "is a unique book in the entire canon of the New Testament."[1] While Acts bears similarities with the Gospels and the New Testament letters at times, its uniqueness lies in its being interpreted eyewitness history (see Luke 1:1–4 for Luke's own statement about this in his work). In this way, Acts is like the four Gospels in giving an eyewitness account of historical events—and yet, no other Gospel writer besides Luke continued the story with a second volume telling what happened after Jesus' earthly ministry. This is where Luke's two-volume work (Luke–Acts) continues the story of Jesus into the era of the early church with its particular interpretation of the ongoing, eyewitness history.

There are many clues that Acts presents us with interpreted eyewitness history. First, Acts intentionally starts and ends at certain significant points: It opens in Jerusalem (the religious center of Judaism) and closes in Rome (the political center of the Gentile world). It starts with Jesus and ends with Paul, the apostle to the Gentiles. It moves from the center of Jewish religious life in the temple to the center of Gentile political life in the capital city of the Roman Empire. This is an intentional decision on Luke's part to highlight the progression of the Gospel of Jesus to the world.

Second, Acts carefully documents specific people, places, and times. Luke is meticulous about including the titles or positions of authority (or lack thereof) held by certain characters, especially those of important Romans. The reason for this is important for understanding his message. The people and places we encounter in Acts aren't just for historical accuracy. Luke mentions them in order to give the story of Acts a particular thrust. Luke wants us to recognize, with historical authority, the emergence of the church in the world beyond Judaism's ethnic and religious boundary markers.

Third, Paul's conversion is recorded three *different* times (Acts 9; 22; 26). If Luke were simply recording history chronologically, then it would not make sense to rehearse the same event multiple times. So why does he do so? Because Luke is *interpreting* certain events with a specific reason or purpose. And he includes particular events, like Paul's conversion, multiple times in particular places for emphasis—it marks the importance of that event in his telling. The conversion of Paul, the apostle to the Gentiles, is key for the spread of the Gospel to the Gentiles.

Fourth, while Paul's letters show the early churches around the Mediterranean as struggling with their diversity (e.g., 1 Cor 1:10–17), Acts consistently emphasizes unity among the churches, though spread across a wide geography. Luke or Paul (or both) have reasons for putting things in a certain light, for telling the story from a particular angle. That is to say, there's more going on than *mere* recording of history. Acts is history with a rhetorical purpose. It's trying to do something to and for the reader. Luke wants us to catch the signal that, despite the diversity of the church, they were unified around their confession of faith in Jesus.

And, fifth, a full third of Acts is taken up by recounting—in detail—sermons, speeches, and other forms of proclamation. What's so important about what was *said*? How many history books tell histories by retelling the speeches that were given? Luke surely must have a reason for doing this—and in Acts, proclamation serves a unique function in the history of the early church. As Paul will write to the Romans, "faith comes from hearing the message, and the message is heard through the word about Christ" (Rom 10:17 NIV). This verbal proclamation is important to Luke, so he takes up a lot of space recounting what was *said*.

For these reasons, it's important to remember that Acts is not only history but *interpreted eyewitness* history. Acts was written by a particular human author, to a particular audience, for a particular reason, to communicate a particular message. Paying close attention to this is important for understanding the message Luke crafted with the inspiration of the Holy Spirit.

Author

Strictly speaking, the author isn't identified anywhere in the book of Acts. So why do most readers and scholars believe Luke is the author, and what do we know about him?

We can conclude that Luke authored Acts, in addition to the Gospel that bears his name, because of the shifting pronouns in Acts. After the opening verses of Acts, in which the author speaks as "I," Acts is entirely written in third person ("he," "they," etc.) except for three sections where "I" or "we" returns (Acts 16:10–17; 20:5–21:18; 27:1–28:16).

SHIFTING PRONOUNS IN ACTS

"In the first book, Theophilus, *I* wrote..." (Acts 1:1)	"So when *they* had come together, *they* asked him..." (Acts 1:6)	"When he had seen the vision, *we* immediately tried to cross over to Macedonia..." (Acts 16:10)	"After they had given *them* a severe flogging..." (Acts 16:23)

If you place these first-person sections alongside the corresponding letters of Paul, you'll notice right away that Luke, "the beloved physician," is present in both (Col 4:14; see also 2 Tim 4:11; Phlm 24). Luke, the faithful companion on some of Paul's missionary journeys, is the best candidate to have written the first-person perspective in these sections of Acts. Therefore, since the earliest days of the church, Luke has traditionally been considered the author of Acts.

But we don't know much about Luke beyond a few educated guesses. He was likely a Gentile—Luke is not a Jewish name. He was probably Roman, because he draws on detailed knowledge of Roman cities, officials, and rulers. His Greek is also rather academic—beyond the level of other New Testament authors, who likely did not have Luke's level of education. Despite probably being a Gentile and a Roman, Luke also displays an extensive knowledge of the Old Testament—especially, as we will see, the ways in which the fulfillment of Old Testament messianic prophecies prepares for the advent of Jesus Christ. This level of familiarity may mean Luke was a God-fearer (a Gentile drawn to the worship of Israel's God but not circumcised) or Jewish convert (a circumcised Gentile). Finally, it's important to remember that although Luke was a first-century physician, his profession would have varied greatly from today's medical doctors'. While some preachers may refer to him as "Dr. Luke," and rightly so, a first-century physician was not a modern-day neurosurgeon.

Date

Unfortunately, there isn't clear consensus on when Luke wrote Acts. There is very little information on which to base a precise date, so nailing one down is like trying to piece together a jigsaw puzzle without knowing what the finished picture should look like or if all of the pieces even are present.

One of the clearest ways to date a New Testament document is whether it refers directly or indirectly to the Jewish War of AD 66–70 and the destruction of the Jerusalem temple in AD 70, a worldview-shattering event for the Jewish community. Unfortunately, Acts can't be dated this way because after the initial chapters in Jerusalem, Acts is primarily concerned with the missionary spread of the gospel beyond Jerusalem. So it makes sense that Luke doesn't mention the destruction of Jerusalem, even if it happened at or before the time of his writing.

Therefore, Acts must be dated by comparing the Roman rulers who appear in the story with extrabiblical records of their reigns. This avenue for dating Acts is quite clear. Most scholars believe Acts was written no earlier than AD 60. This date references the reign of the Judaean procurator Porcius Festus, who died in the early 60s—see Acts 24:27–26:32. On the other end of the timeline, Acts was probably completed no later than AD 90, the latest time by which news of the destruction of Jerusalem would have been known throughout the Roman Empire. This would place the date of Acts' authorship near the end of the first generation of Christians up to the end of the second generation of Christians.

But dating Acts is not only an academic enterprise. It's also important for understanding and appreciating the religious and cultural context from which Acts emerges. The first generation of Christians was very different from today's believers. We must remember that in the events narrated in Acts, Judaism and Christianity were not as distinct from each other as they are today (see Acts 25:19). At first, Christianity was perceived to be a contentious branch of Judaism. Nearly the entire early church was Jewish until Paul's missionary encounters with receptive Gentiles brought surprising ethnic diversity into the life of the church; the debate in Acts 11 is important in establishing the grounds for this diversity.

Also, as Christianity moved into the public world of the Roman Empire, the lordship of Jesus Christ was an entirely new announcement. Although the 1st and the 21st centuries were/are both highly religiously diverse, the first century was pre-Christian, while our century is post-Christian. Also, whereas Christianity has come to fit quite comfortably within many 21st-century cultures, it was the object of intense and sustained persecution in the 1st century. We see in Luke's description of Paul that suffering was the normal state of affairs for Christians in the early church. Reflecting on the dating of Acts helps us to remember the chronological and cultural differences between the context of the book's events and ours.

FIRST-CENTURY JEWISH-ROMAN TIMELINE

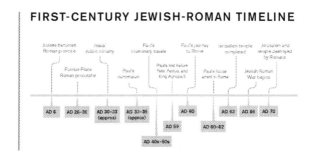

Audience

When someone writes something, he or she usually writes with a particular audience in mind. For whom did Luke write Luke–Acts? We read in Luke 1:3 and Acts 1:1 that Luke is writing to "Theophilus."[2] Some scholars suggest that Theophilus financially supported Luke's research and writing. Others suggest he was a Roman authority who was charged with finding out about this Jesus movement making inroads in the empire. Yet others suggest that Luke compiled the material in Luke–Acts to assist Paul in his Roman trial and that Theophilus was a Roman court official of some kind. Since Theophilus was a common Roman name in the first century, it's difficult to know with any certainty the identity of this particular Theophilus; it could be any number of people.

But maybe it isn't a particular person. "Theophilus," literally translated into English, means "God-lover" ("theo" means "God," and "philus" means "lover"). The tricky part is that "theo" or "god" doesn't automatically mean the God revealed in Jesus Christ, and in the first century, the Roman emperor was considered a god. So Luke may have been evangelistically addressing his Gospel and Acts to "Theophilus"— meaning Romans who needed to hear about the true Lord and God, Jesus. Luke also may have been writing to a Christian audience that wanted to grow in their love for God or know more about God's love revealed in Jesus and announced by the church.

In the end, whoever you are, God is addressing *you* through his Spirit and his Word in Acts. Therefore, as you read through the book, ask yourself: Am I "Theophilus"? Do I love God? Am I ready to hear Acts announce Jesus, through whom I will be loved by God?

Open your heart and mind to what God will say to you through Acts.

> Open your heart and mind to what God will say to you through Acts.

Purpose

Luke doesn't tell us why he wrote his Gospel or Acts (compare John 20:30–31). And yet we can see right away that Acts not only records the history of Jesus' early followers, but that it is also the continuing means by which God transforms people into Jesus' dynamic disciples who will continue to announce God's kingdom.

As a record, Luke's Gospel details Jesus' ministry, while Acts is concerned with the ministry of Jesus' church through the power of the Holy Spirit. This is why a sharp distinction is made in Acts between the Jews who don't acknowledge Jesus as Israel's Messiah and those who do. Jesus is building his church on the fulfilled promises of the Old Testament—with the remnant of Israel and the ingrafted branches of the Gentiles. This also explains why Luke casts the Romans in a positive light. The Roman Empire was the first-century superpower. If Luke wanted the gospel to have an audience within that political context, he needed to demonstrate not only that Jesus was a rival to the emperor, but that Jesus represents something *better* than the emperor.

But in addition to a record, Acts is also the continuing means by which God transforms people into Jesus' dynamic disciples, who will continue to announce God's kingdom. Acts is itself a form of gospel proclamation—it's why Acts is filled with sermons and speeches. We are not only meant to have a record of what was proclaimed, but to hear that proclamation ourselves and respond to it in faith. This is why Acts (like Luke's Gospel) is packed with quotations and references to the Old Testament. Luke shows how Jesus is the fulfillment of God's promises long ago. Jesus is the

> Acts is itself a form of gospel proclamation—it's why Acts is filled with sermons and speeches.

culmination of God's dealings with Israel, and now the church is the beachhead community of God's kingdom on earth, established in Jesus. As Jesus' disciples and God's end-time people, we are not only to respond to the gospel in faith but to take that gospel, like Peter and Paul, and announce it to those around us.

Are you ready to hear that announcement of the kingdom of God in Acts? Are you prepared to respond to the gospel in faith? Are you ready to be a part of the community that takes the gospel to the world? Luke assumes his audience is prepared to say "yes" in faith.

SUGGESTED READING

- ☐ Compare Aristotle's proverb, "Friends hold all things in common" (*Nicomachean Ethics* 9.8.2), with Acts 2:42–47; 4:32–35.
- ☐ Psalm 16 (Psalm 16:8–11 is quoted by Peter in Acts 2:25–28).
- ☐ Deuteronomy 18:15–22

Reflection

What do you think we miss if we read Acts without the context of Luke's Gospel? What difference does it make in how you understand the outline or organization of Acts?

_____

_____

_____

How do you feel about the claim that Acts is not only history, but *interpreted* history? How might we pay special attention to the ways in which Luke, under the inspiration of the Holy Spirit, interprets the historical events he narrates?

_____

_____

_____

Why does it matter who wrote Acts? How does knowing the identity of the author affect our understanding of the divine inspiration of Acts?

_____

_____

_____

Luke wanted to get the history right. But Luke seems to have wanted to do more than only get the history right. Luke also wanted his story of the early church to shape others into Jesus' dynamic disciples. What do you need to do in order to hear and understand the story as Luke tells it? How can it transform your life?

_____

_____

_____

3

KEY CHARACTERS IN ACTS

I was once asked by the local police to serve as a formal witness to a minor crime I had seen happen. This meant that a detective came to my home and asked to take my statement. By "my statement," he meant an official record of what I saw. After I agreed, I was asked many questions about what I saw: Who did it? When did it happen? Where was I when I saw it? The detective wanted detailed facts about the people involved, the scene of the crime, and the dates and times of the event. This is because historical eyewitness accounts of events are important for establishing what really happened.

Those who write eyewitness accounts of history—those who want their accounts to become part of the accepted historical record for generations to come—often take care to include as many accurate details as possible. This is exactly what Luke does in Acts. Acts is filled with the precise names of people, places, and events. Luke shows particular interest in naming the specific people who are part of the early church's story. And Luke *always* uses the proper titles for Roman officials. This displays not only Luke's awareness of how Roman society works, but the care and attention he brings to ensuring his story is accurate. As eyewitness *testimony*, Acts is about real people and real events that occurred. Our question now is: Who are the main characters Luke has included in Acts and what do they contribute to the story?

Collective Character: The Jews

Many individual Jewish people make an appearance in Acts, but Luke uses the collective term "the Jews" more than 40 times throughout the book. To whom is Luke referring?

This phrase, "the Jews," is most concentrated in just a few passages (Acts 9, 13–14, 17–18, and 20–21). These are the places in the story where there is the most conflict between the early church and first-century Judaism. These chapters narrate Paul's initial confrontations with his former Jewish allies (Acts 9), the jealous Jews' plot against Paul when he turns to preach to the Gentiles (Acts 13–14), the Thessalonian and Corinthian synagogues' rejection of Paul (Acts 17–18), and Paul's arrest in Jerusalem before he is deported to Rome for trial (Acts 20-21).

The phrase, "the Jews," therefore, is Luke's way of naming those within the Jewish population who rejected the message about the Messiah Jesus (very clearly seen in passages such as Acts 9:22–23; 12:3; 13:45–50; 14:4). There are only a few exceptions to this overwhelmingly negative usage (Acts 13:5; 17:1, 17; 18:5, 14, 19). In these exceptions, Luke either refers to the generic membership of a particular synagogue as "the Jews" or explains that it was Paul's custom to preach first to "the Jews" before turning to the Gentiles.

In these cases, "the Jews" is just a shorthand way of distinguishing the Jews as a group separate from others, and it doesn't carry a negative overtone. But at all other times, Luke calls those of Israel who are hostile to the gospel message, who persecute the apostles, and who collude with the Romans, "the Jews"—that is, those in Israel who have rejected their Messiah.

In stories of the apostles' conflicts with "the Jews," this phrase often refers to what we would today call "the Jewish leadership." Luke isn't being anti-Semitic by using this phrase, and he isn't implying that all Jewish people rejected Jesus as the Messiah. But in those places in Acts which depict the greatest conflict between the early church and the synagogues, "the Jews" is Luke's way of noting that those in positions of Jewish leadership and influence, who represented the local Jewish community, didn't hear and accept the announcement about Jesus.

"The Jews" were those who orchestrated the same resistance to the early church as had previously been directed at Jesus. It is a designation of unbelief, a religious rebellion against the God of Israel—now the Lord of the entire world—who came in the person of Jesus. But "the Jews" rejected him.

And yet this Jewish rejection is never absolute in Acts. Unbelief is never more powerful than the grace at work in Jesus Christ. In the midst of widespread Jewish rebellion against God's covenant faithfulness, Luke consistently records that some Jews received the proclamation of Jesus as Messiah with courage and joy (Acts 21:20). By and large, "the Jews" is not an ethnic designation but a religious one in Acts.

In the ancient world, it was far more acceptable to group and label people than it tends to be today. It *is* wise for us to be careful when making generalizations about people. But Luke's point about "the Jews" in Acts is that Jesus Christ created a division in the world between those who place their faith in Christ and those who rebel against him (see Luke 12 for Jesus' prediction of this). This cuts across all neat ethnic divisions. When we hear "the Jews" today, it is a challenge to not allow the gospel to go by us without our response of faith. No matter who we are, Jesus is always calling us to follow him with trust and loyalty.

Individual Characters: The Romans

Whereas Luke often refers to "the Jews" as a collective, he never refers to the Romans this way. Rather, he gives unique focus to each individual Roman ruler, official, or citizen in the story. And as Luke's narrative moves from Jerusalem to the Roman colonies to the capital city of the empire, we are introduced to a wide range of characters that gives us a cross-sectional view of first-century Roman society. We meet Roman rulers as well as those who were ruled.

Many Romans responded to the announcement that Jesus was Lord with disinterested aloofness. These Romans believed the message to be of no consequence because, to them, it was abundantly clear who was lord of the world: Caesar. They deemed the announcement of a rival Lord as merely an intra-Jewish debate—of religious significance only. In Acts 18, Gallio, the "proconsul of Achaia," displays this attitude when Paul's preaching in Corinth causes a public riot. According to Luke's narration, Gallio couldn't even be bothered to get involved, telling the Jews to "see to it yourselves" (Acts 18:15). This attitude—disinterested aloofness—was typical of Romans toward all things even remotely Jewish.

Then there are the Romans who became (or were forced to become) very involved in the unfolding drama of Acts due to the nature of their positions. A prime example is Claudius Lysias (Acts 21:33), the Roman tribune in Jerusalem who was charged with protecting Paul against the Jewish leadership's plot to assassinate him—until Paul could be transferred to Rome for trial before the emperor (Acts 23). What's curious about Claudius Lysias is that even though he spends a considerable amount of time with Paul, Luke never records whether he became a Christian. Because of this omission, we can only assume he didn't. But we can also assume that during such intimate dealings with Paul, he would've had the opportunity to hear about Jesus. Lysias is an example of someone who becomes quite aware of the Christian faith (unlike Gallio, who dismisses it immediately out of hand) but never takes the opportunity to invest in it personally. He's just doing his job.

There are also Romans who are downright hostile to the Christian message. For them, Christianity is ludicrous—a form of insanity (Acts 26:24). King Agrippa II is a perfect example of this type of Roman (Acts 25–26). We know from history that Agrippa knew about Judaism and dealt treacherously with the Jerusalem population. Luke vividly characterizes Agrippa, though he speaks of Agrippa's questionable relationship with his sister Bernice with noteworthy modesty. When Paul appears before Agrippa and makes his

defense, Luke records Agrippa exclaiming in response, "You are out of your mind, Paul! Too much
learning is driving you insane!" He then goes on to
dismiss Paul and Paul's announcement of Jesus Christ
by asking the rhetorical question, "Are you so quickly
persuading me to become a Christian?" (Acts 26:24,
28). He then latches onto Paul's appeal to the Emperor
as a convenient excuse to send Paul off to face trial in
Rome (Acts 27). Throughout his encounter with Paul,
Agrippa had ample opportunity to hear about Christ
and to get personally involved, but instead rejected
the gospel.

And, finally, there are Romans who respond to
Jesus in faith. Despite the numerous examples of
Romans who respond to the gospel with quiet disdain
or loud rejection or even disinterest, there are also
those who are drawn to the good news by the apostles'
preaching. These Romans transition from being loyal
to the empire of Rome to being loyal to the kingdom
of God. This is exactly what happens in the life of the
Roman centurion Cornelius (Acts 10). As Luke stress-
es throughout the story of Cornelius' conversion,
from start to finish, the Holy Spirit broke through the

ROMAN EMPERORS DURING THE EVENTS OF ACTS: BEGINNING DATES OF REIGN

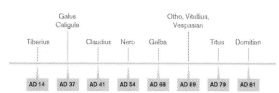

dominating forces apart from Christ that had hold of Cornelius.

But that's how it always is with the proclaimed message about Jesus and the inner working of the Holy Spirit: The result is that God brings about something entirely and unexpectedly new every time.

Majority Characters: Christians of the Early Church

With "the Jews" on their one side and the Romans on the other, the early church—ordinary Christian men and women—actually make up the bulk of the main characters in Acts. After all, Acts is the story of how the Holy Spirit worked in and through these first Christians to give the early church a foothold separate from both the Jewish leadership and the Roman Empire.

Apostles

Jesus called 12 of the earliest Christians to be his disciples and then ordained them as apostles, forming the official foundation of the church—with Jesus Christ himself as the cornerstone (see Eph 2:20). Being 12 in number, they were a highly symbolic group, representing the renewed Israel of God: forgiven, returned from exile, and restored as God's new creation people.

Following the betrayal and suicide of Judas Iscariot, there was an early debate about who could serve as an apostle. It was decided in Acts 1:21-22 that the apostles—as eyewitnesses of Jesus' incarnate ministry from baptism to ascension—were marked out as special. Not just anyone could presume to be an apostle. It was an office rooted in a personal encounter with

Jesus and the communal nature of the church under his leadership.

Even though all 12 apostles were ordained and commissioned by Jesus through his Spirit, Luke's narrative focuses on only a few of them. The early chapters of Acts record the activities of John, James, and Philip, but Peter is granted the most attention. Following his introduction in Acts 9, Paul comes to dominate the storyline from Acts 13 onwards.

It's worth noting that Paul doesn't fit the traditional requirements of apostleship in the same way as Peter and the other 11—and he doesn't appear in the lists of apostles in either Luke 6 or Acts 1. And yet we consistently follow the earliest of Christians in calling him an apostle (something that Paul also seems to wrestle with personally—see Acts 14:14, where Luke refers to Paul as an apostle, as well as the opening verses of Romans, 1-2 Corinthians, Galatians, Ephesians, Colossians, and the letters to Timothy and Titus and compare these with 1 Corinthians 15:9, where Paul calls himself "the least of the apostles"). It is true that Paul witnessed the resurrected Jesus in his conversion (Acts 9) and this qualifies him as an apostle, granted his uniqueness.

As eyewitnesses of Jesus' entire ministry, the apostles are foundational in the sense that they personally experienced the fulfillment of Israel's hope. They received the revelation of God firsthand, from God incarnate himself. As the earliest and most intimate followers of Jesus, they were in a special position to inaugurate the mission of the church to Jerusalem, Judaea and Samaria, and the ends of the earth. Their testimony is the link between Jesus himself and his worldwide following through the ages.

DISCIPLES BECOME JESUS' APOSTLES

During Jesus' Public Ministry (Luke 6:14–16)	After Jesus' Ascension (Acts 1:13, 26)
Simon Peter	Simon Peter
James and John (sons of Zebedee)	James and John (sons of Zebedee)
Andrew	Andrew
Philip	Philip
Bartholomew	Bartholomew
Matthew (aka Levi)	Matthew (aka Levi)
Thomas	Thomas
James (son of Alpheus)	James (son of Alpheus)
Judas (son of James)	Judas (son of James)
Simon (the Zealot)	Simon (the Zealot)
Judas Iscariot	Matthias

Early Christian Leaders

But it's not as though the apostles alone exercised early church leadership; many other leaders accompanied them. It is important to note in this regard that as the witness of the early church moved beyond Jerusalem and into Gentile territory, the nonapostolic leadership in the early church took on a decidedly multiethnic character.

Take, for example, the first deacons as record-ed in Acts 6. There had been a conflict about the fair distribution of church resources between the Jewish and the Greek widows. In response, the apostles des-ignated five men to oversee this important function. Their names reveal that the majority of them were Greek—an important signal that divisions over eth-nicity within the church were addressed by appoint-ing multiethnic leadership.

The same ethnic diversity can be seen in Paul's traveling companions (Timothy and Erastus in Acts 19:22; Gaius and Aristarchus in Acts 19:29; Sopater, Secundus, Tychicus, Trophimus, and some of the others mentioned earlier, in Acts 20). Despite strong roots in Judaism, the church of Jesus Christ transcends ethnic divisions, even at the level of lead-ership. The reason for this, we quickly discover, is be-cause the church is not just the renewed Israel, but the renewed creation. All are wel-comed into the new-creation people of God—as converts, as supporters, as missionaries, as companions on the gospel journey, and even as leaders. Jesus has no privileged ethnic group in his church.

> All are welcomed into the new-creation people of God—as converts, as supporters, as missionaries, as companions on the gospel journey, and even as leaders.

But serving in early church leadership didn't equate with worldly forms of success, com-fort, or ease. Many of the apos-tles and other early church leaders met an untimely death. The world was not receptive to Jesus or his fol-lowers who shared the gospel. The Jewish leadership stones Stephen (Acts 6–7). Herod kills James (Acts 12). And Paul receives beatings and imprisonment in nearly every town he visits. And yet they all received this ill treatment from the world with joy, for it meant that they were worthy to suffer for their faithfulness to the world's true Lord.

Even those who are not recorded as having died as martyrs risked their personal safety and comfort in faithfulness to the Lord. Think of Barnabas— wealthy supporter of Paul's missionary journeys (Acts 4:36–37)—and his bravery in bringing the newly converted Paul to the apostles (Acts 9:27). His action must have struck fear into the hearts of those in attendance that day because everyone knew of Paul's extremist reputation. He was deadly. That kind of news, now as then, travels fast and strikes the heart. In response, some fear and fret. Others follow in faith. The early Christian leaders knew whom they served— no matter the cost.

Other Early Christians

Throughout Acts, Luke is careful to mention by name those who make up the new little churches throughout the ancient world. Each of these people—who are oftentimes the ones who appear the most insignificant at first—plays a unique role in the story of the gospel's spread. Take, for example, Tabitha (also called Dorcas), a Christian believer in Joppa who dies in Acts 9. By raising her from the dead, Peter not only returns her to her important place in the community (note Luke's comment that "all the widows" in her community displayed the clothes she had made, Acts 9:39), but she proves instrumental in spreading the gospel throughout that entire region (Acts 9:42). She was key—in life and in death and in life, again.

Or think of Aquila and Priscilla, the Jewish refugees Paul meets in Corinth after Emperor Claudius expelled them from Rome in AD 49 (Acts 18). Since they share the same trade as Paul (making tents—or, as some suggest, sails), they enter into a partnership—both in business and in Christian mission. In fact, after traveling with Paul on his missionary journeys, they are the ones who mentor a young, eager Christian convert, Apollos, who goes on to teach many about the Christian faith. Some even believe he is the mysterious author of the New Testament letter to the Hebrews.

Conversion isn't just an occasional occurrence in Acts. The book is filled with convert stories—as one would expect in a good missionary narrative. In the case of many of the converts, we never meet them by name (think of the thousands converted in the first few days after Pentecost), but a few are recorded for their significance: the Ethiopian eunuch (Acts 8:26–39), Aeneas of Lydda (Acts 9:32–35), Lydia of Thyatira (Acts 16:11–15), Dionysius the Areopagite (Acts 17:34), and the leader of the Corinthian synagogue, Crispus (Acts 18:8).

Collectively, the many converts recorded by Acts show that, from the very beginning, the gospel was a message for *everyone*: Jew and Gentile, African and European, rich and poor, powerful and powerless, significant and ordinary. There is not a boundary the gospel message does not cross in order to bring about conversion and new life. Rather than a random list of persons, Luke has strategically catalogued the redemption of large swaths of the ancient world—in all of its ethnic, social, cultural, and religious diversity. The gospel of Jesus Christ is for the whole world!

Although the gospel is often received in Acts with much joy, Luke has included three tragic stories of deception by those who hear the gospel: Judas Iscariot in Acts 1:18; Ananias and Sapphira in Acts 5:1–10; and Simon the magician in Acts 8:9–25. These three stories are included as instances of a *lack* of faith among those who hear the gospel message and in some way participate in the early church. Their stories are ones of betrayal, deception, and selfish pride in the early days of the church. The church is *not* a conflict-free zone; these stories remind us that from the earliest days, faith has been accompanied by unholy motives, that the human heart is rebellious against God, and that sin is destructive. Even today, we ought to lament the brokenness that exists in the church—but we should not be surprised by it.

Main Character: The Holy Spirit

Many human characters make an appearance in Acts but none of them can truly claim to be the *main* character. That position can only be rightly attributed to the Holy Spirit—the one promised by Jesus in Luke 24:49 ("I am sending upon you what my Father promised; so stay here in the city [Jerusalem] until you have been clothed with power from on high"). The Spirit is sent to believers in the opening chapters of Acts.

The Holy Spirit directs activity throughout Acts, dispersing the apostles with the gospel. The Spirit works behind the scenes in every unfolding development. The Holy Spirit is the living presence and power of Jesus in the unfolding life of the Christian church.

In Acts 2, the Holy Spirit arrives and commissions the apostles for their missionary work. In Acts 4, the Spirit emboldens Peter to preach that Jesus Christ is the fulfillment of God's Old Testament promises. In Acts 5, Ananias and Sapphira's lie about their offering to the church is a "lie to the Holy Spirit" (5:3); the Spirit is intimately united to the church. In Acts 6, the selection of the first deacons is based upon the Spirit being alive in them. In Acts 7, the Spirit stands with Stephen and gives him the words to speak before his martyrdom. In Acts 8, the Spirit goes before the apostles to open their imaginations to the wideness of their missionary calling. In Acts 9, the Holy Spirit leads (another) Ananias to Paul, following Paul's encounter with the risen Jesus. In Acts 10, the Spirit falls upon Gentiles, astounding the Jewish Christians. In Acts 11, the Spirit is the source of Agabus' prophecy. In Acts 13, the Holy Spirit sets aside Paul and Barnabas from the Antioch church to depart on a missionary journey. In Acts 15, the Holy Spirit guides the Jerusalem council to include the Gentiles in the church. In Acts 16 and 19, the Holy Spirit directs Paul in his missionary travels. In Acts 20, the Holy Spirit guides Paul to Jerusalem even though it will mean his arrest.

In all these ways, and many more, the Holy Spirit is the main character in Acts. The Holy Spirit guides the church, directs the church's missionary travels, confirms the expansion of the church into uncharted territory, and encourages believers in the face of rejection and persecution. At every important point in the advance of the gospel throughout Acts, the Holy

Spirit leads God's people forward. All the other characters
in Acts merely respond in faith
(or rebellion) against the leading of the Spirit.

> At every important
> point in the
> advance of the
> gospel throughout
> Acts, the Holy
> Spirit leads God's
> people forward.

Readers of Acts then or now,
observing this Holy Spirit-
church dynamic, are chal-
lenged to decide how they will
respond to the Holy Spirit. We must ask ourselves:
Am I receptive to the Holy Spirit's leading in my life?
What would faithfulness to Jesus, under the direction
of the Holy Spirit, look like in my life, job, or neigh-
borhood? What gifts has the Spirit given me, and
where is he guiding me to use them? These are the
kinds of questions Acts provokes for its readers in all
times and places. In other words, do we have ears to
hear and hearts to respond? The good news is that the
Spirit is always present with Jesus' followers, is always at work for God's purposes in the world, and is
always bringing new life out of human dead-ends.

SUGGESTED READING

- ☐   Acts 8:26–40
- ☐   Acts 9:32–43
- ☐   Isaiah 2:1–4

Reflection

As noted in this chapter, "the Jews" refers to those of the Jewish leadership who did not believe that Jesus was Israel's Messiah. Who in your culture is most likely to reject the message of Jesus while also having the leadership capacity to influence others against Christianity? How can the church today proclaim and display the love, joy, and truth of the gospel to these unbelieving leaders?

_____

_____

_____

In Acts, Luke displays a detailed knowledge of the Roman Empire and its rulers, customs, and beliefs. Why do you think such detailed knowledge was important in the historical and cultural context of the early church? What was the benefit for the church to have this knowledge? How do we benefit by knowing these kinds of details about our own cultures today?

_____

_____

_____

The gospel is for everyone—that's one of the lessons we learn from the different Christian converts in Acts. But to whom do we still struggle to bring the gospel? Who do we sometimes think is beyond the pale of the gospel?

_____

_____

_____

How do you feel knowing that the story of the early church also includes tragic elements—such as instances of lack of faith?

_____

_____

_____

Do you agree that the Holy Spirit is a "character" in Luke's story of the early church? Do you think there's a better way to think of the presence and role of the Holy Spirit in the church? How do you understand the Holy Spirit's relationship with the church today?

_____

_____

_____

4

CONFLICT IN ACTS

Acts tells the story of how the Holy Spirit propels the apostles—and many other characters—in the development of the early church, as we saw in the last chapter. But as the apostles encounter the world outside the church (whether in Jerusalem or a far-flung Roman outpost), stories of opposition, rejection, and even persecution are just as common as conversion to faith in Jesus. Why is Acts filled with so much conflict? Nearly every chapter of Acts includes a story of misunderstanding, struggle, persecution, arrest, or even death.

This is *not* what we would normally expect after such a positive beginning following Jesus' resurrection and ascension. Why must the spread of the gospel be linked so closely with conflict?

Along with many others, I've wrestled with this issue myself. I remember when, as a university student, I was asked to be part of a panel discussion on Christianity. At the event, it soon became clear that the panelists had been invited in order to debate the role of the church in civil society. At the time, I was a Christian leader on campus, so the event coordinator likely assumed I would argue that the church is called to convert the world to Christianity in a crusading, forceful manner.

The panelists represented a wide variety of positions. One or two advocated that the church should stay well out of politics; another spoke from an atheistic position; still another represented a more pietistic Christian tradition. One panelist believed the church was a humanitarian agency that should seek to promote peace and harmony among conflicting groups. Someone else felt that the church should get with the times and support popular hot-button political issues. I decided to mix things up a bit, so I argued the church is a witness to Jesus Christ and that role of witness is a public role rather than a private one; the result of this witness is that the church provokes conflict in society. Like Jesus, the church takes a stand, which often results in divisions and conflicts.

I don't know if I won anyone to Christianity that day. My strategy may have been all wrong. But I do know one thing: Acts supports my argument, because one of the book's more surprising themes is conflict.

Many people have an idealistic view of the early church. As God's people—restored through Christ and witnessing throughout the world—the early church is assumed to be a kind of utopia for later generations to emulate.

> The early church is definitely a prototype, but not of conflict-free community.

The early church is definitely a prototype, but not of conflict-free community. Jesus came and drove a wedge between faith and unbelief (see Matt 10:34). The church in Acts finds itself in the midst of these same divisions. Stories of betrayal and deceit accompany stories of conversion and expansion. The early church found itself embroiled in conflict at every turn; the gospel consistently provoked conflict.

The conflicts in Acts fall into three types: the church in conflict with (1) the Jewish leadership; (2) Rome; and (3) itself. Let's take an in-depth look at passages that masterfully tell these stories. Lingering in the background of each we'll find important and practical questions for ministry today: What are the parallels to these conflicts in my own setting? What does faithfulness to Christ call for in the midst of this particular conflict? Make no mistake: Christians all have to grapple with conflict at some point. The question is whether that conflict will be about the gospel message itself, or some Christian's muddleheaded obnoxiousness.

The Church in Conflict with the Jewish Leadership (Acts 3–4)

Acts begins in the most explosive way: Jesus' resurrection and ascension, the coming of the Holy Spirit, the preaching of the gospel at Pentecost that converts thousands, and healings.

And then Peter and John are arrested for saying and doing these things in the "unauthorized" name of Jesus, Israel's Messiah. The teaching and the healing in Jesus' name in Acts 3:1–4:22 displays the initial conflict between the early church and the Jewish leadership, particularly the temple leadership. It's written as a unit. Note the literary bookends of the section: Acts 3:1 opens with the story of the beggar's healing; Acts 4:22 closes the section with the astonished crowd's summary remarks about the beggar.

What is the cause of the conflict?

The apostles were speaking and acting *in the name of Jesus* (Acts 3:6; 4:7, 10). They were claiming that what was traditionally understood to be obtained through the temple—forgiveness, holiness, connection with God—could now be obtained through Jesus, a would-be Messiah who had been recently executed. To complicate matters, Jews in first-century Jerusalem knew that if they needed healing, the temple was the place to go. And yet, here were the apostles circumventing the temple, offering people the temple's goods without the authorization of the temple leadership. Their actions, done in the name of Jesus, were rendering the temple unnecessary, obsolete, and powerless. By objecting to the actions of the apostles done *in the name of Jesus,* the temple leadership were objecting to the claim that Jesus was the promised Messiah and that he superseded the temple. The apostles' actions were highly symbolic: They called the entire Jewish tradition into question in light of Jesus. The apostles were redefining what faithfulness to God entailed. And that caused intense conflict with the Jerusalem (temple) leadership.

But there's an additional angle to the cause of this conflict. Why has this crippled beggar, who has obviously been outside the temple at the Beautiful Gate for some time, never gone into the temple to obtain the healing he so clearly needs? The most obvious answer is because, as a crippled man, he is ceremonially unclean—and therefore prohibited from entering the temple.

But the more subtle answer is that he's a beggar. He doesn't have the funds for the required offering associated with healing in the temple. He's doubly excluded from the temple and therefore from God's presence and the presence of his community. He lacks *all* the means by which to live a full life in fellowship with God and God's people.

So the apostles—by healing the beggar outside the authority of the temple—are not only circumventing the religious rules of the day; they are also subverting the crippling economic system of the temple (pun intended!). This crippled (read: undeserving) beggar received healing for free! The apostles' words and actions are the equivalent of Jesus turning over the money changers' tables in the temple! Here, grace functions as an economic threat as well as a religious one.

What is the nature of the conflict?

From a religious perspective, the apostles' teaching and healing ministry proceeded without authorization from the temple leadership. They based their actions on Jesus' authority instead. From an economic perspective, the apostles subverted the temple's unjust system, which welcomed some and excluded others; the apostles' lives were ones of radical grace, mercy, and hospitality.

But let's be clear: The apostles did not base their actions on some political agenda, but *in the name of Jesus*. The apostles' actions symbolically stated that Jesus had superseded, even replaced, the temple when it came to faithfulness to God. Their message— the gospel—was this: In Jesus' resurrection, God's long-awaited redemption and new creation had begun. The temple leadership had missed this message

> In Jesus' resurrection, God's long-awaited redemption and new creation had begun.

when they turned Jesus over to the Romans for crucifixion. And now they were being confronted again with a claim that they lacked faithfulness to God—the very thing on which they were supposed to be experts and of which they were supposed to be guardians. Their power (see Acts 4:7) was being critiqued. But they weren't going to take that sitting down; thus ensued conflict with the early church.

How does the church respond to the conflict?

Peter and John were under intense pressure—direct orders, in fact—"not to speak or teach at all in the name of Jesus" (Acts 4:18). There are always times and places where the culture surrounding the church would like the church to keep quiet about Jesus, especially when he calls for repentance and life changes. The early church and the church today are in strikingly similar positions in this regard. How did Peter and John respond?

First, they recognized that faithfulness to Jesus outweighed the need to meet expectations from earthly authorities (Acts 4:19-20). Second, they brought the conflict to the wider Christian community for further discernment (Acts 4:23-31). The wider Christian community affirmed Peter and John's actions as correct; then, together, they praised and thanked God, and the Holy Spirit ministered to them so that they could withstand the cultural pressure to keep quiet.

Note here that this conflict arose because of who Jesus is, not the apostles' methods of proclaiming Jesus. Too often Christians mistake unbelievers' objections to Christian methods as objections to Jesus himself. It is important for the church in every age to proclaim Jesus in such a way that any objections are to Jesus' message rather than to the methods used to share him with others.

> It is important for the church in every age to proclaim Jesus in such a way that any objections are to Jesus' message rather than to the methods used to share him with others.

What is the result of the conflict?

This initial conflict results in greater and more intense conflict between the early church and the temple leadership. The conflict moves from arresting, questioning, and threatening to active persecution in the span of a single chapter (Acts 5). Faithfulness to Jesus does not guarantee a comfortable life or cultural success. While initially Jesus' followers were viewed as a pesky sect of Judaism, the formal rift between the two communities became inevitable and stark (as documented in Acts 3–4). By Acts 8, the Jewish leadership is proactively seeking out and rounding up Christians by going door-to-door. They send a network of Jewish messengers to all the diaspora communities around the ancient world, warning them about the Christians. And as Acts unfolds, we see the Jewish leadership colluding with Roman authorities to forcefully stamp out the Christians. Through it all, this conflict actually solidifies the early church's identity and mission in Jesus Christ.

What does the conflict reveal about God and/or the gospel?

The apostles believed that Jesus was the fulfillment of the Old Testament promises to Israel and that Jesus therefore replaced the Jerusalem temple and its sacrificial system. As Israel's Messiah, his sacrifice rendered the temple and its sacrificial system unnecessary and ineffective. The entire system's purpose in God's covenant was fulfilled by the ministry of Jesus— forgiveness and restoration is available to the people of God directly through Jesus in the power of his Spirit. The presence of God is now found in the midst of his people, where the Holy Spirit resides.

We also learn from this conflict that Jesus is the absolute Lord of the whole world. And Jesus leads his church to engage the world with the message about his lordship. The church is called to bear that message into the whole world, through numerous gifts and tasks. But while Christian faithfulness is important, it is Jesus who is the head of the body, the Church, and it is his project to renew his creation, forgive his people, convert his elect, and restore all things. Ultimately, the work of redemption is God's.

Finally, this conflict teaches us about the nature of the church. The church is not just a bunch of individuals thrown together. Rather, it is an organic community woven together by the faith bestowed by the Holy Spirit. This is an important point because many modern Christians live in highly individualistic cultures.

The church may exist in many local communities and denominations, but as the community of all God's redeemed, the Church transcends ethnic, cultural, linguistic, economic, and political divisions as a single family knit together by God's Spirit. The Church is the sign of God's kingdom present in the world. It is a community that experiences joy from proclaiming the gospel, courage from the Spirit's presence, and conviction in standing for Christ against all other rival claims.

The Church in Conflict with the Roman Empire (Acts 10)

In today's world, religious conflicts often turn into political conflicts. The same was true in the ancient world: The early church had to contend with Jewish leadership on one side and Roman authorities on the other. In Acts 10, we get a glimpse into Jewish life under Roman occupation and the church's navigation of that conflict.

Acts 10 tells of the apostle Peter and the Roman centurion Cornelius. Peter represents the church under Roman occupation, and Cornelius is the powerful face of that occupying force. The Spirit of God intrudes into each of their lives with visions and direction, cutting through the boundary lines between Jew and Gentile, clean and unclean, Israel and Rome, Christian gospel and Roman military dominance. Unlike Acts' many tragic stories about the church's conflicts with the Roman Empire, the story in Acts 10 has an encouraging resolution—even if it's not completely neat and tidy.

What is the cause of the conflict?

At first glance, there doesn't seem to be any serious conflict in Acts 10. But when we look deeper, we may see a significant conflict going on in the background of the encounter, and it's all about power: the power

KINGDOM OF HEROD

of the gospel versus the political, military, economic, and cultural power of the Roman Empire. It is a conflict between oppressed and oppressor.

Luke provides many hints that point to this reading of Acts 10. In 10:1 we learn that Cornelius is a centurion, a Roman military officer. But more than that, he is of the "Italian Cohort" (a special military division) stationed in Caesarea (literally, "Caesar's city"). Luke portrays Cornelius as the kind of man who has power—power to send, summon, command, order, and direct. By contrast, Acts 10:5-6 portrays Peter living by the sea, away from the big city and its influence. It's a humble picture of the margins of society, with the stench of death—rotting fish—constantly filling the nostrils (which would have made Peter ceremonially unclean for worship in the Jerusalem temple, too!). Peter is depicted, in light of the Roman Empire's power, as the kind of man who's only good for obeying orders.

The Roman Empire was a foreign—pagan and Gentile!—force in Palestine. The Romans were idolaters in the Lord's holy land. Rome's occupation of Palestine shows the long-term results of Israel's failure to take their promised land by conquest or to heed the words of the prophets so many generations before. As the early church emerged out of Judaism—a faith that insisted upon strict separation between Jew and Gentile—the church began dealing with how to relate to this historical and political situation (namely, the Roman enemy breathing down their necks).

But the larger question here is not just about religious stipulations in the face of unbearable political imposition. The question concerns how the church will respond to a host of alien and hostile powers in the world. Will the church adopt the same stance of separation and enmity—possibly even armed rebellion—as the Jerusalem leadership? Will the church take up armed resistance like other Jewish factions? The sheer power imbalance between Peter and Cornelius sets the stage for little more than the same oppressor-oppressed relationship between the two.

What is the nature of the conflict?

This conflict is about power. Rome seems to have all the power to impose a particular status quo—even on the church—and there doesn't seem to be any way out of it. But this forces us to ask a deeper question: What kind of power does the church exert? Is the power of the church the same kind of power as the Roman Empire's? Does the church's power just take a different form than the empire's?

If the power of church and empire is of the same flavor, end of story. Rome will squash the church if it's purely a contest of muscle. If it isn't, maybe a new future is possible with God—if the church has a power unique from that of the empire.

Luke consistently presents Peter as a preacher of the gospel. Nothing more, nothing less. And we know from Luke's hints and from history that Rome was a brutal power that oppressed many so that a few could live in the lap of luxury. And yet, in Acts 10, we see Peter and Cornelius both claiming to follow a ruler with the title "Lord." Both Caesar and Jesus have taken that title for themselves. Cornelius has money, might, and means. Peter has a message from Jesus. What could the gospel possibly offer Cornelius, who so clearly has everything he needs at the snap of his fingers?

The answer gets at the nature of the conflict between them: It is a conflict about whose form of power is faithful to God's creation.

How does the church respond to the conflict?

Undeterred by the power imbalance, the church responds with faith—expressed through the proclamation of the gospel. Peter, as an apostle of the early church, doesn't attempt to meet the power of the Roman Empire on its own terms. But neither does Peter transform the message of the gospel into something that he expects Cornelius would find more palatable, acceptable, or attractive (note the near-rudeness of Peter's opening remarks in Cornelius' household in Acts 10:28–29). This isn't promotional or attractional ministry. Peter is a witness, not a salesman. Do you feel the suspense building throughout the encounter in Acts 10?

Central to Peter's sermon at Cornelius' house is verse 38: the message of "how God anointed Jesus of Nazareth with the Holy Spirit and with power; how he went about doing good and healing all who were oppressed by the devil, for God was with him." This verse falls at the literary center of Peter's sermon and contains two references to power, though one is lost in many English translations.

Peter first refers to the power of the Holy Spirit, which anointed Jesus at his baptism. This is a clear reference to Jesus being the Old Testament's foretold Anointed One, the Messiah. But the second reference to power in this verse is translated as "oppressed."

It's from the same Greek word as the power of the Holy Spirit mentioned before, but here it's the negative form of the word, thus carrying the dominating negative side of the word's meaning. And Peter says that this is the power of the devil—which Jesus negates through his healing and liberating grace.

Who might Peter have in mind when he speaks of the oppressive, dominating power of the devil? That's right: Caesar and the oppression of the Roman Empire all throughout Judaea. Peter isn't just talking about an unseen spiritual battle between invisible forces. He's speaking on Cornelius' level: on the level of actual, historical, embodied forces of good and evil. So Peter's message to Cornelius is that Jesus, in the power of the Holy Spirit, would liberate Cornelius from the oppressive power of Roman rule and life (a form of life in league with the devil) if he would simply repent, believe this good news, and shift his life's allegiance.

The church's response to such power dynamics isn't to draw back, circle the wagons, and withdraw from the thorny political issues of the day. Rather, the church courageously and faithfully responds by proclaiming, in context, the gospel—a gospel that is able to speak to every issue faced by fallen humans. The gospel for Cornelius, for Rome, or for any empire is that worldly power that uses force to oppress and dominate others runs against the grain of how God created the world to be—a place

> The church courageously and faithfully responds by proclaiming, in context, the gospel—a gospel that is able to speak to every issue faced by fallen humans.

of peace, justice, and righteousness. But an alternative is possible (in fact, already is present) through Jesus, who heals human rebelliousness and leads the way to the fullness of flourishing life. Peter doesn't hesitate to name death and the devil where they exist in their historical manifestations. But he also responds in a redemptive manner that leaves room for God to do his converting work through the Holy Spirit. Having heard the church's proclamation, Cornelius now has a choice to make: Remain in rebellion and under the domination of the devil's forces, or change allegiances through the power of the Holy Spirit and encounter true human life the way God intended.

What was the result of the conflict?

Peter was faithful to his calling, and "while Peter was still speaking the Holy Spirit fell upon all who heard the word" (Acts 10:44). The result of this conflict was that God burst into the midst of the gathering and broke the impasse, issuing in redemption, conversion, and fellowship across previously impermeable lines.

Luke uses few words to communicate the result of Peter's proclamation and Cornelius' conversion, but those few words display a remarkable shift for the unfolding history of the early church. First, the church formally welcomes Gentiles into their fellow-ship—into the family of God (see Acts 11)! Today we might miss the outrageousness of the time-honored Jewish boundaries between Jew and Gentile, but they are astonishingly—recklessly—crossed by the Holy Spirit through the gospel.

Second, we have the initial fulfillment of what Luke has been driving at up to this point in the story of Acts: the worldwide reach of the gospel to transform the whole world.

Third, this encounter foreshadows and opens up Paul's missionary journeys to the Gentile lands beyond Palestine.

And finally, this passage points us to the conclusion of Acts, when the gospel message reaches the very heart of the Roman Empire, the capital city (see Acts 28:30–31). Just as Peter the Jew travels to preach the gospel to Cornelius in Caesarea, so also Paul the Jew will travel to the heart of the Gentile world to preach the gospel. Their preaching eventually reveals the weakness and foolishness of the Roman Empire—overthrowing its grip on the oppressed through the love and grace of God.

What does the conflict reveal about God and/or the gospel?

The power of the Roman Empire and the power of the gospel are very different. Through this conflict, the gospel's power is distinguished from the political and military power of the state. The church's power of proclaiming the gospel lies not in its ability to mimic the power of Rome but in its ability to point to the One who liberates and heals those under oppression. The church often runs into trouble precisely when it lusts after or seeks powers that have been granted to other social institutions and authorities in human life. This is nothing less than a lack of faith in the gospel. It's a lack of courage in proclaiming that Christ is indeed Lord of all.

But the conflict between Peter and Cornelius also reveals the central role of gospel proclamation in the life of the church. Gospel proclamation is not a nice extra, tacked on to the church's ministry when possible. Gospel proclamation is not a booster rocket that gets the church going before the church turns to other things to maintain its life and ministry. No, gospel proclamation is the very lifeblood of the church, the means by which Jesus dwells among his people.

Peter faced a significant temptation when meeting with Cornelius: to trade the true gospel for a false version that he imagined would appear more relevant or attractive to Cornelius. The church today often faces this temptation. Many gimmicks claim to help build or manage the church more effectively. But when the church's time, attention, effort, and resources are monopolized by such ideas, what is left for proclaiming the gospel? The church's ministry, too, can become a source of oppression if it isn't clearly rooted in the gospel.

Finally, this passage teaches us that even when the church's missionary efforts are directed to the hearts of individuals, we still must keep the wider social or institutional context in view. The proclamation of the gospel isn't only for individuals; it is also meant to shape the whole world—communities, institutions, and cultures. The Christian faith should propel believers out into the world so we rub shoulders with all sorts of people engaged in all sorts of activities in all sorts of cultural arenas. Ideologies and idolatries exist on an individual level as well as on social and institutional levels. All need to be countered with the liberating grace of Jesus Christ.

Every Christian is a missionary because Christianity is a missionary faith. It is a faith that doesn't live cloistered and huddled behind safe walls. Rather, it goes public, right under the noses of the power brokers of every culture and society. And the church is called to proclaim—and equip others to proclaim—this *comprehensive* gospel.

> Every Christian is a missionary because Christianity is a missionary faith.

The Church in Conflict with Itself (Acts 5)

In a church I once pastored, a member came to me one day to let me know that a particular extended family in the congregation was not on speaking terms. Decades earlier, an older generation in this family had passed away and the estate had been divided up unequally, or so it was alleged. Even 20 years later, this event still kept the family apart. There had been no reconciliation, and it seemed there never would be. Money conflicts like this are, unfortunately, all too common in middle-class suburban churches.

The early church wasn't a utopia of pristine faith and mutual love, either; members of the early church had their own money conflicts. The story in Acts 2:44-47—where "all who believed were together and had all things in common"—is the exception, not the rule. Acts 5, a haunting story about Ananias and Sapphira's deceit, is just one example of the conflict the church experienced within itself. Like today, however, money was only the surface issue; the real issue lay deeper in the heart of the church. And at times, the intense conflict present in the church's inner life became a life-and-death matter.

What is the cause of the conflict?

Ananias and Sapphira had some disposable income, a portion of which they gave to the church. But they claimed they had given *all* they had when in fact they had only given *some* (Acts 5:1-2). They lied to the Holy Spirit (Acts 5:3, 9). They were entirely free to give any amount they wanted; Peter says so in Acts 5:4. What was unacceptable was their lie, intended to make themselves appear more generous than they actually were. The money was only the husk around the kernel of a proud heart. The conflict began when the lie began. And the lie began when pride took up residence in their hearts.

What is the nature of the conflict?

To answer this, we must remember two important Old Testament stories: 2 Samuel 6 (the death of Uzzah while transporting the ark) and 2 Chronicles 26 (the death of King Uzziah after an unauthorized sacrifice in the temple). Both of these stories hinge on the issue of pride. Uzzah was proud and thought he could offer help to the wobbly ark. Uzziah was proud and thought he didn't need the temple priests as middlemen for his piety and worship.

These stories make Acts 5 understandable. The church is the presence of God in the world, like the ark, tabernacle, and temple before it. No longer does God dwell in a golden box or a golden temple, but in the midst of his people by his Spirit. Therefore, to play games with the church as if it were merely another human community is to tread carelessly on holy ground. To place one's self above the church is to place one's self above God. Therein lies Ananias and Sapphira's tragic end.

How does the church respond to the conflict?

It is critical to note that Peter does not carry out the death penalty. Luke intentionally says that upon hearing Peter's acknowledgment of their sin, both Ananias and Sapphira "fell down and died" (Acts 5:5, 10), implying that it was entirely God's action. The church, in the person of the apostle Peter, recognized the lie, but the Lord carried out the judgment.

This distinction is very important. The church, when it perceives that it has been wronged—or when it actually has been wronged—often feels compelled to not only name the wrong but also to carry out the appropriate punishment. Acts 5 shows that while Ananias and Sapphira did wrong, the church wasn't responsible for dishing out the consequences. Rather, the church—like Jesus—absorbs the wrong, suffers the wrong, and leaves the judgment and punishment to God. This is not to say that there aren't natural consequences (often to safeguard those who have been victimized from further harm or abuse). But the church must be cautious about identifying itself with God and presuming what God would do. It's too easy for a wronged church to go on a crusade of its own agenda and thereby perpetuate the wrong rather than provide healing.

What is the result of the conflict?

The immediate result is that "great fear seized the whole church and all who heard of these things" (Acts 5:11). Why does Luke introduce *fear* here?

Through the first four chapters of Acts, incredibly wonderful things are happening: The Holy Spirit has come, thousands are being converted to Christ, people are being healed, authorities are being resisted, and the church is living joyfully. It's easy to imagine how this could lead to a misplaced triumphant attitude: "Look at what we're doing! We're turning the world upside down!"—which isn't too far from "we're so great!" And then pride, which has been ushered out the front door, slips in again through the back door.

This kind of attitude turns Jesus into a tool we use or a power we control to accomplish our desires and goals in the world of our own making. The story of Ananias and Sapphira reminds us that this community of the new creation, the church, belongs to Jesus and is to be approached and treated with respect and reverence. The respect and reverence is not for the church leadership per se, but for the Spirit of Jesus in their midst. The church is not a human accomplishment. It is the result of God's redemptive activity in the world. And that divine activity, because it is renewing and redeeming all things, deserves appropriate respect. Otherwise, we may forget who we're dealing with—and before we know it, we're justifying a whole host of sin this way. The note of fear here keeps "look at all this great stuff happening around us!" from becoming "we're so great!"

What does the conflict reveal about God and/or the gospel?

Acts 5 reveals the depth and complexity of human sinfulness, which God addresses through the gospel. Humanity's rebellion against God is not only seen in heinous, large-scale acts of genocide, embezzlement, or human trafficking, but also in the small motivations and actions that flow from a sinful or rebellious heart. These are the things that can reveal dangerous self-deception among Christians. At times, our rebellion against God may be so subtle that our true motives may be hidden even from ourselves. As broken people following Jesus, it's all too easy to condone one sin with a wrongly motivated act of piety. God, by his grace, is working to address and heal even this level of rebellion within us.

But in Acts 5 we also learn that our compartmentalization of life, which is still quite common, is arbitrary and self-serving. This conflict reveals that there is, in fact, a deep connection between our church life and our financial life. Jesus does not call us to follow him with only part of who we are (for example, our "hearts"), leaving other parts of who we are (for example, our financial transactions) walled off from the call to discipleship. Everything in our lives reveals the state of our faith—not only the worn edges of our Bibles and our raised hands in worship. This can be particularly challenging for middle-class North Americans comfortable in lives filled with possessions—which blind them to their privilege and lead them to neglect justice for the downtrodden. Everything matters when you're following the Lord of everything.

To wrap up, I invite you to reflect on how Acts 5 sums up the argument Luke has been making from the beginning of his Gospel (volume one) right through to the opening chapters of Acts (volume two). The presence of God in the world that was once located in the ark of the covenant or the Jerusalem temple has become incarnate in Jesus of Nazareth. Now, with Jesus' ascension and the outpouring of his Spirit on the church, the church is a unique body on earth. It exists in two modes: as a gathered community under ordained leadership and as a sent/scattered body—individuals or voluntary organizations—

> The presence of God in the world that was once located in the ark of the covenant or the Jerusalem temple has become incarnate in Jesus of Nazareth.

that seek to bear witness to the gospel in the whole of life. The church is not primarily a social club, a justice advocate, a civic morality police force, or even a humanitarian agency. In the church community, the presence of the world's Creator, Redeemer, and Sustainer is present and active. To lightly or flippantly play games with God, while dwelling in this community, may be utterly disastrous.

SUGGESTED READING

☐ Isaiah 60–61

☐ 2 Samuel 6

☐ 2 Chronicles 26

Reflection

How does the church today call the reigning authorities' rules for life and society into question? How should the church exercise its prophetic critique of power today?

In Acts, the church is in conflict with the Jewish temple leadership. But today, this is not the church's primary religious conflict; today, the church's greatest threat comes from alternative religions and worldviews. What can we learn from the church's conflict with the Jewish leadership for our own interactions with other worldviews today?

Compare and contrast Peter's ministry to Cornelius with your church's ministry with people today? Does your church rest secure in the power of God working through foolishness and weakness? Or does your church seek to adopt the forms and the exercises of power that are commonplace in the world outside the church? What do you think Peter would say about your church's way of carrying out its ministry?

_____

_____

_____

Peter preached to Cornelius in such a way as to safeguard Cornelius' freedom to choose his response to the gospel. How can our outreach and evangelism avoid manipulation or coercion and leave our friends with a genuine choice between life or death?

_____

_____

_____

How do you feel about what God did to Ananias and Sapphira? Why, exactly, does this sin receive such an immediate and drastic response? What do you think is the root of the ongoing conflict between money and the church?

_____

_____

_____

How do you hear "the fear of the Lord"? What does it mean, in the specifics of your life, to revere and/or respect the Lord? How does one actually do that?

_____

_____

_____

MAIN THEMES
IN ACTS

When I was in high school, I was one of the yearbook photographers. Every day I endured the snickers of my peers as I carried a 35mm camera with me everywhere I went. I took pictures of everything: sports events, students in the library, teachers in their labs, graffiti that mysteriously appeared on the bathroom walls.

One of the things I liked most about being a school photographer was the many angles to choose from when taking a picture. I could take a close-up of the popular couple kissing in the stairwell, or a panoramic shot of the stands at the Friday night football game. Each perspective offered a unique glimpse of high school life.

When you decide to study a book of the Bible, you have a similar choice of perspective. You can take a close-up look at the details or a wide-angle view of the big picture. You can move verse-by-verse in focused study, or you can pull back and look at the overall textual patterns.

In chapter three, we took a close-up look at the characters in Acts. In the previous chapter, we began to view Acts in panorama mode to see some of the book's big-picture themes. We'll continue with this wide, sweeping view and examine the other primary themes in Acts—they will give us a stronger framework with which to understand the many stories and events that occur over these 28 chapters.

Fulfillment of Scripture Prophecy

Luke must have loved the Old Testament. He quotes and alludes to it often. For example, in the first four chapters of Acts, he makes direct reference to the Old Testament no less than 10 times (and alludes to it another 9 times). Luke shows how the prophecies of the Old Testament are fulfilled in Jesus, in the coming of the Holy Spirit, and in the birth of the church.

But this pattern isn't limited to the first four chapters. Acts is filled with references to the Old Testament. And with each quotation of Old Testament prophecy, Luke demonstrates that Jesus is indeed Israel's Messiah, the world's true Lord, and that the church is the outworking of God's long road of redemption.

Luke wrote two volumes for a good reason: to show not only the fulfillment of Old Testament prophecy in Jesus, but also to show the fulfillment of Jesus' own prophecies in the church for the renewing of the world. At the close of Luke's Gospel, Jesus says "that repentance and forgiveness of sins is to be proclaimed in his [the Messiah's] name to all nations, beginning from Jerusalem" (Luke 24:47). Then Acts tells the story of how the gospel is proclaimed to the entire world, starting in Jerusalem and eventually stretching to the far reaches of the first-century world. Each phase of Acts' storyline charts the progressive spread of

REFERENCES TO THE OLD TESTAMENT IN ACTS

Acts	Old Testament
2:17–21	Joel 2:28–32
2:25–28	Psalm 16:8–11
2:34–35	Psalm 110:1
3:22–23	Deuteronomy 18:15
4:11	Psalm 118:22
7:56	Daniel 7:13–14
8:32–33	Isaiah 53:7–8
13:33	Psalm 2:7
13:34	Isaiah 55:3
13:35	Psalm 16:10
13:41	Habakkuk 1:5
15:16–18	Amos 9:11–12
17:31	Psalm 9:8
26:23	Isaiah 42:6

the gospel through the apostles' missional activities. Luke maps a first-century Jew's entire known world, right up to the political center: Rome itself (Acts 28). In this way, Luke demonstrates how Jesus fulfills Old Testament prophecy and how the church fulfills Jesus' own prophecy.

Word and Deed Proclamation

But Acts not only narrates the proclamation of the gospel by the early church's missionary journeys. It is also, itself, a form of the gospel's proclamation—showing the fulfillment of prophetic Scripture and reaching through the centuries right to today. But Acts isn't just about *words*. The proclamation of the gospel also involves symbolic and powerful *deeds*.

Modern readers may wonder why Luke includes so many miracles in his story of the early church (e.g., Acts 3:6–7; 5:12; 8:13; 9:17–18, 32–35, 40). In the modern world, many readers may not experience the miraculous in their lives in the way presented in Acts. They may even be suspicious about miracles.

But miracles, according to Acts, aren't just fireworks that make people "ooh!" and "aah!" They are visible attestations of the verbal proclamation of the gospel. They confirm and verify the words as true. For this reason, it makes sense that miracles don't happen all the time and that they are clustered around key points in redemptive history. But in Acts, miraculous deeds go with the words as verification; anyone can claim his or her message comes from God, but the miracles' presence or absence act as proof. We see this also in John 2, where Jesus' miracle at the Cana wedding causes his disciples to believe he is who he said he was. This same idea is also beautifully illustrated in the healing of the paralytic lowered through the roof in Luke 5:11–26.

Luke continues to illustrate this pattern of word and deed proclamation in Acts. Peter heals a beggar in the temple courts to confirm his apostleship and Jesus' lordship (Acts 3). In Acts 9, Paul is healed, confirming Jesus' appearance to him on the Damascus road. Aeneas receives healing in Acts 9:32–35, and this opens the door for the whole region of Lydda and Sharon—which was northwest of Jerusalem—to receive the gospel in faith. Words plus deeds equals faithful gospel proclamation as the Spirit leads the church into new territories.

Even the descriptions of the early church's life (Acts 2:43-47; 4:32-37) function to not only describe the early church's character but to demonstrate that the church is the community of the new creation. The church is the visible confirmation of Jesus' messiahship and lordship. Jesus is the world's true king, as proclaimed by the church (words), because his people, the church, are the visible demonstration of a people who are joyfully loyal to his kingship (deeds). Anyone can claim with words that the Jewish exile is over. But the descriptions of the early church *show* that the exile is over, forgiveness has been granted, and the world has been born again.

> But the descriptions of the early church *show* that the exile is over, forgiveness has been granted, and the world has been born again.

It seems to me that one of the most important ways that word and deed proclamation happens today is when Christians who bear witness to the gospel also bear evidence of the gospel's work in their own lives. Rather than being judgmental and cranky, they demonstrate patient love and gracious hospitality. If the church doesn't display Christlikeness in its common life together, the watching world will see very little evidence that the gospel is true. Without deeds, we have a religious club, not a church.

Public Christianity, Public Church

In many places in the world today, faith is assumed to be a private matter. It's considered personal and, therefore, not intended for expression in the public realm. I experience this regularly as a chaplain on a public university campus; most students and staff assume religious, faith-based, or spiritual activities have no part in the academic mandate of the university. Most expect faith in general—and Christianity in particular—to remain in the parking lot when you arrive on campus. It is assumed that public institutions are "secular" because they don't allow any religious expression.

This so-called "secularism" is a misunderstanding of faith as a core component of one's identity and also displays a prejudiced view of Christianity in particular; it has always been a public faith. Jesus spoke openly—in synagogues and open fields—and not in secret (John 18:20). In Acts, the apostles spoke openly in homes and marketplaces. Paul defends himself before King Agrippa, saying that he did nothing in secret, out of the way, or in a corner (Acts 26:26). Christianity is lived on the public stage of history and society. And the church is not a private sect, huddled away in secret, but a movement that lives out in the open, before rulers and ruled alike. The faith and church illustrated in Acts are embedded in the public arena of the diverse world.

Christianity is public is because Christianity—believed or lived, alone or in community—is comprehensive. It touches all of life. Faith is not a private opinion but a public confession. The proclamation of the gospel is not only for the already converted, but for those living estranged from God. To be a Christian isn't so much a religious or spiritual choice, but a public announcement about who truly rules the world.

The Holy Spirit's arrival at Pentecost happened in the midst of a national celebration (Acts 2:1, 5, 8–9). Peter's first sermon was to a crowded street corner (Acts 2:5–7, 14–36). The early church's first worship sessions took place in the bustling corridors of the Jerusalem temple (Acts 2:46). The gospel is announced in halls of political power (Acts 26). In Acts, every chapter seems to find the apostles in marketplaces or arenas or public courts or busy seaports or pagan lecture halls. The early Christians show us: Christians live "out of the closet."

But because the early church was so public, it also suffered. The apostles were often arrested and put on trial; they experienced muggings, floggings, and even executions. There is hardly a town Paul visits that does not respond to the gospel with fists. For every positive story about the sharing of the gospel, there seems to be a story about persecution.

Several factors contributed to the early church's suffering. The Jewish authorities felt threatened by the claim that they had missed (and killed) Israel's Messiah. The Roman political leaders felt threatened by the claim of a rival ruler of the world. The Athenian philosophers felt threatened by the idea of the resurrection, which called their rationalist theories of reality into question (Acts 17:31–32). The pagan idol merchants of Ephesus felt threatened because their economy was based on the idolatry of Artemis (Acts 19). No status quo was safe. And because the early Christians questioned that status quo, those invested in the status quo responded with violence.

The early church suffered because the gospel they proclaimed addressed the ethnic, religious, economic, political, commercial, and confessional aspects of the world it encountered. People likely would have easily accepted a private, subjective, or personal message that left the status quo untouched. But the gospel, with prophetic power, questioned the fallen world—and so persecution followed. The announcement that Jesus is the world's true Lord was either received in faith or rejected in rebellion. The gospel called the first-century audience—and continues to call us today—to live counterculturally in nearly every possible way. Christianity is a public faith. The church is a public gathering. The gospel is a message about the world. But the world is not naturally inclined to embrace it.

The Kingdom of God

The early church proclaimed a gospel rooted in the fulfillment of Old Testament (and Jesus' own) prophecy. The early church proclaimed a gospel with both prophetic words and Spirit-empowered deeds. The early church was a public movement proclaiming a public message (and, therefore, suffering publically).

> The early church proclaimed a gospel with both prophetic words and Spirit-empowered deeds.

Another way of putting this—in a way that draws all these elements together—is to say that the early church was animated by the kingdom of God. This is the thematic background to everything that happens in Acts; the whole book is only truly intelligible when placed in this context.

In Luke's Gospel, the kingdom (or reign) of God is a major theme (see Luke 4:43; 8:1; 9:2, 11, 60; 10:9, 11; 11:20; 12:31–32; 17:21; 22:29–30). This same focus carries over into Acts: It is what Jesus teaches his disciples before his ascension (Acts 1:3). It is what Philip preached in Samaria (Acts 8:4–12). It is what Paul preached in the synagogues (Acts 19:8). And even in the heart of the Roman Empire, Paul announces a rival kingdom— the kingdom of *God* (Acts 28:23, 31).

What do we discover about the kingdom of God in Acts that opens up our imaginations? First, this is a kingdom that is entered not through birth but through rebirth, or repentance— literally a turning from one life-direction (in rebellion against God and conformity with the fallen world) to another (compare John 3). In contrast, becoming a Roman citizen in the ancient world required a significant financial purchase if one was not born into privilege.

Throughout Acts, the apostles teach that the kingdom of God is life lived liberated from enslavement to self-destructive beliefs, attitudes, and habits. This is why Jesus can proclaim that faith in him leads to an abundant life (John 10:10). On the other hand, the Roman Empire allowed a special few to live in lavish comfort and debauchery while the unfortunate masses lived as slaves, enduring grueling labor and poverty.

The kingdom of God is a joyful rule of mercy and grace. The Roman Empire ruled with an iron fist of inflexible law often upheld through extreme punishments. In fact, the Romans crucified so many "lawbreakers" (real or accused) that the executioners could hardly keep up with the demand.[1]

The kingdom of God's advances in the world are achieved through love: fellowship meals, kind words, compassion to neighbors, generosity. In contrast, the Roman Empire advanced through an army equipped to the teeth with the most technologically advanced weapons, the most ruthlessly calculated strategies, and the meticulous management of resources, human or otherwise.

In all these ways, the kingdom of God as revealed in Acts is the whole world's true goal. The kingdom of God is *the* picture of the world redeemed, liberated, and given a new lease on life. Acts contrasts these contours of the kingdom of God with the fallen forces of the world, which are alienated from God. The kingdom of God is the hope of the entire world.

In the part of the world where *you* live, what do people assume to be the hope of the world? A political party? Financial success? Fame, or comfort, or health? Keep your answer in mind as we move forward to consider how to read and apply Acts today.

SUGGESTED READING

- ☐ Amos 9:11–15
- ☐ Acts 9:1–19
- ☐ Habakkuk 1:1–11

Reflection

Prophecy is often thought of as foretelling the future. With the fulfillment of Old Testament prophecy in Jesus, how does Acts direct us in understanding the role of prophecy in the life of the church today?

_____

_____

_____

Word and deed are linked because the deed verifies the truth of the word. Can you think of some other reasons word and deed are important to consider together, rather than as separate aspects of how we live out our faith as either individuals or as church communities?

_____

_____

_____

Acts shows the persecution of the church. Why are or why aren't we persecuted today? Does persecution automatically mean faithfulness? Why or why not?

_____

_____

_____

If you live in a democracy, it might be hard to visualize the kingdom of God. What does it mean to be a citizen of a kingdom? How is it different from being a citizen of a democracy?

_____

_____

_____

As the church has grown as an institution, it has tended toward an inward focus. How can we balance care for and nurture of the inner, institutional life of the church while being careful not to neglect the outward, public-engaging ministry of the church?

_____

_____

_____

READING AND APPLYING ACTS TODAY

Inevitably, at some point, the announcement that Jesus is Lord leads us to face the question, "Now, what am I going to do about it?" The same is true with Scripture in general and Acts in particular. It's not enough to leave the biblical text in the ancient world. We must do the hard work of carrying the text over a great historical and cultural distance for it to have application in the life of faith today. In the process of connecting Acts to our present context, one of the key factors for us to remember is that the first generation of the church lived in a *pre*-Christian time, while we live in a *post*-Christian time.

The Missionary Journey Continues

We have thoroughly considered the beginning of Acts—so let's turn now to the ending of Acts. At the end of the book, in Acts 28, you may feel as though you're left hanging, wondering, "What happens next?" It doesn't *feel* like a conclusion: Acts ends with Paul in Rome under house arrest, but continuing to freely preach the gospel right under Caesar's nose. It's unsatisfactorily open-ended.

Luke most likely does this intentionally, both as part of his rhetorical strategy and in alignment with the way he has crafted Acts' narrative. In ending the book this way, he reminds us that the missionary journey is never truly done. From the very beginning, Christians have boldly taken the gospel to the very ends of the earth. Luke doesn't chart the missionary journey of the early church up to a tidy completion because the missionary journey of the church will always continue.

Today, therefore, we should finish reading Acts inspired to embark upon the missionary life that marks the identity of a Christian believer. But after 2,000 years of Christian missions, there are fewer and fewer places that have yet to hear the gospel. Today's Christians live in a highly mobile society; thus, while all Christians today should have a missionary mindset, it may not result in moving halfway around the world. It might mean proclaiming the gospel in our own cities and towns. Global missions is becoming local missions.

> Global missions is becoming local missions.

Modern Christians, animated by the message of Acts and compelled to share the gospel in their own contexts, will need their churches and other Christian organizations to disciple and train them in how to verbalize and demonstrate the joyful message that abundant life can be found in Jesus. In North America and Western Europe, for example, many generations of Christians have been content to live as if Christianity provided the foundational beliefs and social morals of society and to financially support a small group of others to leave home for faraway places as full-time vocational missionaries. We've accepted our cultural Christianity, our civic religion, without much fuss or questioning.

Christians, churches, and Christian organizations must recognize the radically changed environment we inhabit. The mission field is just one step out our front doors. We're all called to bivocational missions now. We're all part of the continuing missionary journey that started in Acts. Are you ready? If not, what do you need to do to be prepared?

The Church's Power Temptations

Part of being prepared to bear witness to the gospel today is knowing the dynamics of our world. Early Christians knew the religious and political landscape of their time, and they were able to navigate it and communicate the message of Jesus within it. We must do the same today. We must know the world we are surrounded by, its forces, ideas, and assumptions.

As 21st-century Christians, we may be tempted to overlook—or push aside without enough critical discernment—various aspects of our world. For instance, we may not pay attention to the extent to which our world is permeated by forms and networks of power. Large-scale forces get much attention in the media: transnational global capitalism, the military-industrial complex, national or ethnic ideologies, commercial advertising, welfare-state entitlements, and technological surveillance. But smaller-scale, less institutionalized influences are nonetheless powerful: social expectations, subcultural customs, familial rules, interpersonal nonverbal signals, and peer pressure. To be human is to be enmeshed in a web of powers and authorities. Sometimes these forms of power are so subtle or so accepted that they become invisible, and we hardly notice their presence in our lives. But they're there, if we know where and how to look.

Christians in the first century also had to navigate forces and networks of power and authority. The powers of money, the state, religion, ethnicity, law, human tradition(s), philosophy, magic, commerce, art, transportation, education, military, medicine, trade, and many others are evident in Acts. Each step of the way, the early church had to discern the presence and nature of these powers' influence and decide how to interact with them in a way that was faithful to the Lord Jesus (who, Paul announces, is Lord over all things and is renewing all things—Colossians 1:15-20). We can see in Acts how all of these powerful forces are, at one time or another, capable of doing much good but also of being distorted for human misery. The faithful Christian discerns the path through them, taking advantage of the powers that contribute to healthy human life and seeking to nullify distorted powers, which can dominate.

For example, take the fact that Paul was a Roman citizen. Citizenship was a significant form of power and privilege in the first-century Roman Empire, especially for a Jew. Roman citizenship was outrageously costly and granted special rights far beyond what ordinary noncitizens were able to enjoy. And yet, throughout Acts, Paul only resorts to his citizenship privileges once—to avoid a public flogging and as a means of appeal to the emperor directly

(Acts 21:37–25:12). All other times, Paul submits to the pain and humiliation that the gospel provokes (see Acts 14:22, where the early church expresses their belief that "it is through many persecutions that we must enter the kingdom of God.")—even though, as a Roman citizen, he could have been excused from that humiliation and pain again and again.

In contrast, many stories in Acts show how worldly power is a destructive temptation: Judas betrays Jesus for money; the Jewish leadership colludes with the Roman authorities to kill Jesus; Ananias and Sapphira lie to the church about their offering; Herod kills the apostle James; Simon the magician tries to buy the power of the Holy Spirit for his own fame. The message of Acts is clear: Worldly forms of power are a destructive temptation for the church and Christians. Instead, the church's unique form of power is its vocation to proclaim the gospel in word and deed, knowing that many will nevertheless view it as foolishness and weakness.

Christians (and the church) would do well today, therefore, to follow this trajectory in adopting a critical and discerning (and probably even healthily indifferent) attitude toward those forms of power, highly prized by our culture, that are actually harmful to human flourishing.

Often those forms of power guarantee technological effectiveness and efficiency—and they are forms of power that Christians have fallen for. For example, the church leader employed by a military equipment manufacturing corporation responsible for what the media often calls "collateral damage" needs to seriously consider where his or her true loyalties lie. The same call for serious introspection applies to the convenience store clerk who sells lottery tickets to those struggling to put healthy food on the table for growing children.

Acts reminds us that being a Christian, being a member of the church, is a serious matter that lays claim to the entirety of our lives. We can not turn a blind eye on the networks of power dynamics all around us—many of which benefit us greatly in a worldly sense, but which also distort how we live created in the image of God—and hope that everything will turn out in the end. Jesus' lordship calls for our deepest loyalty, period.

> Jesus' lordship calls for our deepest loyalty, period.

Private versus Public Faith

Just as Acts challenges our understanding of power, so it also challenges our understanding of church. For some, "church" is a building with a cross on the top, just like a library is a building filled with books for borrowing. For others, "church" is a holy huddle, a group of like-minded folks seeking a safe withdrawal from the evils of the world. For still others, "church" is one option among many—a club to be freely joined or left depending on how one feels but which doesn't have any claim on one's life.

And yet, for a growing number of people today, "church" is simply irrelevant. It's invisible. I remember talking with one pastor who told me a story of a young woman, a local university student, who lived in an apartment just across the street from his church building. She had lived there for nearly four years.

One Sunday morning she heard the church bells ringing, woke up, looked out the window, and exclaimed, "Hey! There's a *church* across the street!" She simply had never noticed that the building across the street was a church—it was a nonentity in her life.

Luke consistently uses the Greek word *ekklesia* to describe the gathered and sent Christian community in Acts. The word literally refers to those who are "called out." In ancient Greece, primarily in Athens, the *ekklesia* was a public gathering of citizens. They were "called out" from their regular lives to perform citizenship duties.

This raises an important question: Why does Luke and other New Testament authors use this word— such a *political* word—for Jesus' followers? We don't often think of the church as the gathering of the citizens of the kingdom of God, but that's the word's original intent. The church is the citizenry of the new creation.

The roots of this usage can be found in the Old Testament, in the people of Israel gathered before God, who was present in their midst in ark, tabernacle, and temple. This means that the church is the gathering of Christians before the presence of God, revealed in Jesus in the power of the Holy Spirit. And the Lord Jesus sends the church into the world with the gospel. This is what makes the church unique in the world: It is the firstfruits of the renewed creation.

But this identity does not remove the public nature of the gathering. The church still meets in the midst of the world. As Paul says in Acts, there is nothing about Christianity or the church that limits their special religious activity to be hidden away from public view, off "in a corner" (Acts 26:26).

Reading Acts today means that we must come to terms with the reality that the church as portrayed in Acts is always a visible entity. It is a public rather than a private gathering. The church lives its life on the open stage, before the eyes of the world. Yes, it lives its life with a unique identity, but that identity separates the church from sin and rebellion against God, not from God's creation.

The missionary nature of the church in Acts bears this out even more clearly. The church is sent into the whole world with a message about the world's true Lord. That is a public claim about reality, not a private matter of religious opinion. The church does not exist in secret. It does not profess secret beliefs. It is the visible gathering of those who, by faith, have been born anew into the citizenship of the kingdom of God.

Together for the World

The church in Acts is public. It adopts a discerning attitude toward the fallen world. It is always engaged in mission. The church in Acts, therefore, is together for the world. The church is the dynamic people of God living together for the world. This is what captures the plot, themes, and overall purpose of Acts. This is the "big idea."

> The church is the dynamic people of God living together for the world.

Acts tells the story of the early church: Jesus' ascension; the coming of the Spirit; the apostles' witness in Jerusalem, Judaea, and Samaria, and all across the ancient world; the founding of churches in every village, until the gospel makes its way to the heart of Rome. This is the geographic expansion of the church.

But there's also the emergence of Christianity from within Judaism and the separation of the church from the Jerusalem temple. All Gentiles are welcomed: Africans, Asians, and Europeans; slaves and free; men and women; rich and poor. There is hardly a socioeconomic or ethnic boundary line that the gospel doesn't cross. This is the cultural expansion of the church.

And as the early church expands—geographically and culturally—it encounters resistance, rejection, and persecution. The history of the early church is not painless. The church consistently suffers physically, emotionally, financially, socially, and politically. But this never renders the gospel null and void; the sufferings of the church to bring the gospel to the world actually spotlight the church's witness to the kingdom of God, the truth of the gospel, and the reality of Jesus Christ alive and at work by his Spirit. Counterintuitively, this captures the kingdom expansion of the church. It is a unique and puzzling kind of expansion for the fallen world to understand apart from faith because it is an expansion accomplished through weakness, foolishness, struggle, and sacrifice. This is because it is the work of God, rather than of sinful humanity.

Remember God's call to Abraham millennia ago. God promised that he would bless Abraham in order that all the families of the earth would be blessed through him (Gen 12:1-3). As the story of Abraham is recorded for us, God's promise to him doesn't mean his life was easy, painless, comfortable, or "successful."

Just the opposite is true: Abraham's life was marked by deep doubt, intense struggle, and painful dependence. But Abraham faithfully followed God's promise.

Abraham trusted God and believed God to be faithful—and yet his experience of walking into the unknown future was likely that of walking into a fog. But through Abraham's dependence upon God, God worked his purposes out for the world in the establishment of Israel and the coming of the Messiah, Jesus. In his Gospel and Acts, Luke records for us how God brought Israel's (and, therefore, human) history to its fulfillment in Jesus, who bestowed his Spirit on his people and sent them as his dynamic church into the world with a message of salvation and ultimate blessing.

Acts, therefore, tells the story of the church being *together* for the world. Acts is a story of those called by God out from the mass of sinful humanity to faith in Jesus Christ, the world's true king. This church, being called out, is then sent back into the world as missionary and ambassador, to proclaim in word and deed the reality of the kingdom of God.

But Acts is also a story of the church sent *into the world*. The church isn't called to a holy huddle, a circle of wagons, or a defensive fortress against the sinful world. Rather, the church is the vanguard of a movement that's living and active, oriented toward the world beyond the church's boundaries. The church is that gathered and sent company of heavenly citizens who live in allegiance and loyalty to Jesus Christ and who permeate every part, aspect, and arena of the world with a contextualized message of love, joy, and hope. The world is in rebellion against its Creator, Redeemer, and Sustainer, but the church brings the world an announcement: New life is available through repentance and conversion to Jesus Christ. Just as God so loves the cosmos (John 3:16)—the entire created reality—so, too, the church is also called to love the world, through words and deeds, enough to suffer the birth pangs of God's incredible grace, which is causing the world to be born anew.

This is the story of Acts: the story of the church, as the dynamic people of God, going to the world, for the world. Reading Acts today, just as in the first century, we are invited to follow Jesus, in the power of his Spirit, into his world. That might be far away; it might be next door. But we are called to take up the gospel and be caught up in the expansions of the kingdom of God.

We are witnesses. We don't do this alone, but in the company of all of King Jesus' loyal subjects and the presence of the King's Spirit. And we are promised that we will never be left as orphans along the journey. For the King's name is Immanuel-God with us and, through us, with the world.

SUGGESTED READING

☐   Genesis 1:26–31

☐   Revelation 7:9–17

☐   Isaiah 58:1–14

Reflection

How do you feel about the claim that all Christians today are missionaries, called to announce the gospel in word and deed to the diverse people who fill our neighborhoods, workplaces, and communities?

_____

_____

_____

What do you need from your church to equip, support, and encourage you in your bivocational missionary life and work?

_____

_____

_____

What forms of cultural power do you or your church have? How can you cultivate those gifts for the flourishing of the immediate area of your home, workplace, or church building?

_____

_____

_____

When you think about the church today, does it seem like a public or a private entity? What happens when the church withdraws from the public stage? How might your church need to change in order to more closely align itself with the model of the church in Acts?

_____

_____

_____

BIBLIOGRAPHY

Recommended Scholarly Works on Acts

Barrett, C. K. *The Acts of the Apostles: A Critical and Exegetical Commentary.* Vol. 1. London: T&T Clark, 1994.

———. *The Acts of the Apostles: A Critical and Exegetical Commentary.* Vol. 2. London: T&T Clark, 1998.

———. *Acts: A Shorter Commentary.* London: T&T Clark, 2002.

Bruce, F. F. *The Book of the Acts.* The New International Commentary on the New Testament. Rev. ed. Grand Rapids: Eerdmans, 1988.

Fitzmyer, Joseph A. *The Acts of the Apostles: A New Translation with Introduction and Commentary.* New York: Doubleday, 1998.

Gonzalez, Justo L. *Acts: The Gospel of the Spirit.* New York: Orbis Books, Maryknoll, 2001.

Pervo, Richard I. *Acts: A Commentary.* Minneapolis: Fortress Press, 2009.

Talbert, Charles H. *Reading Acts: A Literary and Theological Commentary on the Acts of the Apostles.* Reading the New Testament. New York: Crossroad, 1997.

Walaskay, Paul W. *Acts.* Louisville: Westminster John Knox Press, 1998.

Witherington, III, Ben. *The Acts of the Apostles: A Socio-Rhetorical Commentary*. Grand Rapids: Eerdmans, 1998.

Suggested Pastoral Commentaries for Teaching and Preaching on Acts

Fernando, Ajith. *Acts*. NIV Application Commentary. Grand Rapids: Zondervan, 1998.

Keener, Craig S. *Acts: An Exegetical Commentary.* 3 vols. Grand Rapids: Baker Academic, 2014.

Pelikan, Jaroslav. *Acts: Brazos Theological Commentary on the Bible.* Grand Rapids: Brazos Press, 2013.

Stott, John. *The Message of Acts: The Bible Speaks Today*. Downers Grove: InterVarsity Press, 1994.

Willimon, William H. *Interpretation: Acts*. Atlanta: John Knox Press, 1988.

World Council of Churches Publications. *Spirit, Gospel, Cultures: Bible Studies on the Acts of the Apostles.* Geneva: World Council of Churches, 1995.

Wright, N. T. *Acts for Everyone: Part 1 and 2*. Louisville: Westminster John Knox Press, 2008.

Background Resources for the Study of Acts and the New Testament

Carson, D. A., and Douglas J. Moo. *An Introduction to the New Testament.* 2nd ed. Grand Rapids: Zondervan, 2005.

Carson, D. A., Douglas J. Moo, and Leon Morris. *An Introduction to the New Testament.* Grand Rapids: Zondervan, 1992.

Evans, Craig A. *Ancient Texts for New Testament Studies: A Guide to the Background Literature.* Peabody, MA: Hendrickson, 2005.

Klein, William W., Craig L. Blomberg, and Robert L. Hubbard, Jr. *Introduction to Biblical Interpretation.* Nashville: Thomas Nelson, 2004.

Longman III, Tremper, and Raymond B. Dillard. *Introduction to the Old Testament.* 2nd ed. Grand Rapids: Zondervan, 2006.

NOTES

Chapter 1: Introduction

1. For more on this idea, see F. F. Bruce, *The Book of the Acts*, in the New International Commentary on the New Testament (Grand Rapids: Eerdmans, 1988), 3–5.

2. This theological claim is based on the overall message of multiple passages, such as Matthew 5–7, Ephesians 3, and Colossians 1.

Chapter 2: Background to Acts

1. Justo González, *Acts: The Gospel of the Spirit* (Maryknoll, NY: Orbis Books, 2001), 1.

2. The literature on Theophilus is vast. A good summary from respected evangelical scholars is D. A. Carson, Douglas J. Moo, and Leon Morris, *An Introduction to the New Testament* (Grand Rapids: Zondervan, 1992), 195.

Chapter 5: Main Themes in Acts

1. The ancient Jewish-Roman historian Josephus writes of how the Romans crucified hundreds of Jews in the Jewish-Roman War of AD 66–70 in order to try and psychologically manipulate them to surrender (*Jewish War* 5.11.1, section 449–451).